Disorder

PHOENIX POETS

VANESHA PRAVIN

Disorder

THE UNIVERSITY OF CHICAGO PRESS

Chicago & London

VANESHA PRAVIN teaches at the University of California, Merced.

The University of Chicago Press, Chicago 60637
The University of Chicago Press, Ltd., London
© 2015 by The University of Chicago
All rights reserved. Published 2015.
Printed in the United States of America

24 23 22 21 20 19 18 17 16 15   1 2 3 4 5

ISBN-13: 978-0-226-23536-3 (paper)
ISBN-13: 978-0-226-23553-0 (e-book)
DOI: 10.7208/chicago/9780226235530.001.0001

Library of Congress Cataloging-in-Publication Data

Pravin, Vanesha, author.
    Disorder / Vanesha Pravin.
        pages ; cm. — (Phoenix poets)
    ISBN 978-0-226-23536-3 (pbk. : alk. paper) — ISBN 0-226-23536-x
(pbk. : alk. paper) — ISBN 978-0-226-23553-0 (e-book)
    I. Title. II. Series: Phoenix Poets.
    PS3616.R388D57 2015
    811'.6—dc23

                                        2014041295

for my mother, HEMLATA, *and my father,* PRAVIN

CONTENTS

ACKNOWLEDGMENTS

Grateful acknowledgment is made to the editors of the following journals, in which some of the poems first appeared, some in different forms:

Callaloo: "Hemma Remembers Disorder" (under the title "Disorder") and "Hemma Remembers Two Cities" (under the title "Two Cities")
Crab Orchard Review: "Sleep, Wake, Sleep"
Many Mountains Moving: "Sweet Milk"
Slate: "City Aubade"

The translation from the *Upaniṣads* on page 57 that introduces "Pomegranate" is by Patrick Olivelle (Oxford: Oxford University Press, 1996).

Special thanks to Robert Pinsky for his support over the years, and for providing many insightful suggestions on earlier versions of the manuscript. Thanks also to Louise Glück for many valuable suggestions on a number of the poems in the book, and to the anonymous readers for providing additional feedback. I am also grateful to Maggie Dietz for her encouragement and insight, and to Laurel Ann Bogen for first teaching me how to "find" the poem. In addition, I'd like to thank Martha Sholl and Carl Johnson, who provided me with the room where much of this book was written from 2008 to 2009. My dear friend Elizabeth Appleby was an ongoing source of support during the long process of seeing the book come to fruition, and for that I will always be extremely grateful. I would also like to thank my father, Pravin, and my mother, Hemlata (Hemma), for sharing the family history that inspired many of these poems (although creative license has been taken), and for first encouraging me to write. And finally, this book could not have been written without my wonderful husband, Rolf, who provided extensive feedback in addition to his unwavering love and support.

I

THE PHARMACIST'S HOUSE

Haverhill, MA 2008

I.

September again and a new
Old house, a rag in my hand,

Dusting my sandalwood elephant,
And the tusks fall into a gap

Between pine planks.
Down there, Carl found

Trading cards of boxers
From 1910—Stanley Ketchel

And Owen Moran, born like me
In Birmingham, and a scrap from

The New York Ledger I read in
Late afternoon sun. A pharmacist,

Michael Flynn, owned the house then.
Centiliter markings reaching 440

On bottles dug up in the garden.

II.

I'll live here for a year.
The winter will be

Long, the snow heavy.
And oftentimes,

Nothing to say, no one
Speaking, I'll doodle

Flynn's medicinal bottles
On credit card statements.

III.

Mumbai and the man
Held the tusks

To my eyes, showed
How to slide them

Into the elephant,
Wrapped them

With care in a
Scrap of newspaper.

IV.

The New York Ledger,
Saturday August 19,

1871: But it may be said
Literature is to catch

And copy the features
Of actual life. We say Yes

… with reservation.

FIRST WIFE

for my great grandfather Harilal

Areca nut crushed with tobacco,
    clove and cardamom,
lime and fennel seeds
    wrapped in a betel leaf,
Kunku folds the paan

and brings it to Harilal,
    the railroad conductor.
She sits with him, the sun
    a pink eye
low over dry fields.
    Kunku gazes at it.

Boys on rooftops
    are flying kites,
Harilal chewing
    slowly, spits.
His teeth, his gums,
    the ground
stained with the bright
    red of paan.

Happy red, color of
    love, of prosperity,
union of betel and areca nut.
    Kunku cannot conceive.
It is spring, Harilal is forty.

MIDSUMMER

Cambridge, MA 2008

Midsummer. Finally, you are used to disappointment.
A baby touches phlox. Many failures, many botched attempts,

A little success in unexpected forms. This is how the rest will go:
The gravel raked, bricks ashen, bees fattened—honey not for babes.

All at once, a rustling, whole trees in shudder, clouds pulled
Westward. You are neither here nor there, neither right nor

Wrong. The world is indifferent, tired of your insistence.
Garter snakes swallow frogs. The earthworms coil.

On your fingers, the residue of red pistils. What have you made?
What have you kept alive? Green, a secret, occult,

Grass veining the hands. Someone's baby toddling.
And the phlox white. For now. Midsummer.

SECOND WIFE

for my great grandmother Jiba

The first wife, Kunku, travels
north, closer to the desert
in search of a bride.

There: God and rain,
rice and peace—Jiba, a girl
of 16, a farmer's child

whose father cannot
afford her. Steadfast,
inured to the unexpected,

she had seen monsoons
bend wheat, and water buffalo
die in the rasp of drought.

Kunku makes an offer, the women
return south to become sisters,
slip into a home and share, grinding

red chilies to sell roadside.
They beat wet sheets on rocks,
turn them white, knead wheat flour

with oil, with water. The grain
entwined, bread puffed
over the open flame.

AGAPANTHUS IS THE WORD

Central Valley, CA 2009

It is June. The field
Bleached, monochromatic.

The stubby palms
Fanged, erect.

Lavender buds
You've failed to identify—

Long stems shot forth,
Longest of the street.

You've won.
You've grown something

You cannot name.
Wrists now bolted,

The grass mown, the mind cured.
Some things prove true,

The rest fall wayside.
Years scatter, the sequence blurred,

And the measure is skewed.
The trees fill with obols.

It is June. Let's hope
Someone is kind, just in time.

And the tease, the nubby growth
Reaches forth

To catch its birds,
To catch its birds.

THE ARRANGEMENT

Late afternoons hiss—the two wives simmer
Raw milk and water, with the dust of tea leaves,

With bruised ginger, cardamom, ground peppercorns,
The cloves floating on top, woody and whole.

Hot chai to be drunk under the tamarind, the pods
Phallic, dangling, their pulp used for chutney.

In the evening, the air cool for a walk, Kunku
Leaves Jiba alone with Harilal, whose children

Are born to two mothers. The youngest, a girl—
Her name *Santha* means *calm, pacified.*

THE NINTH FLOOR

Emeryville, CA 2002

The town runs itself, rapids
Of white headlights, dark faces
Folded over steering wheels.

The sky lightens in drawn seconds.
A ringing in the ears. Zigzags
Ripple on the hotel carpet.

Of course, our senses can
Deceive us. Still, you stare and
Stare. A dark habit cuts across glass—

A finite commute into quiet.
The sky, the sky—you cannot
Watch it lighten. Deep blue

Slows the minutes—you drift and
When you emerge, the sky is paler,
Quickening from dark to light.

You've been dissected by time,
Rendered the unreliable witness,
Willing the distant hills to harden.

So, doubt choices, doubt judgment,
Doubt the whole of your life.
How easily you have missed so much.

MORGENDÄMMERUNG
Peaks Island, ME 2008

Pink fans across the
early sky, sharpens
wings in descent,

scratches the eye.
In the tide pools,
the secret lives

of sea urchins.
The gulls darken,
thrust in relief.

INNOCENCE

Santa Fe, NM 2000

We found the endangered:
Mancos milk-vetch,

razorback suckers,
whooping cranes up-

drafted into a curdled hatch
of our mystery play,

a salty rim,
a rooftop cantina,
the rain, the rain!

Laughing
when hail pelts your ear.

Sensation
our equalizer.

———

I kept believing
what you managed,

until the better, darker
equalizer of time.

A logician,
and logical—
you were still wrong.

———

Years later, last night:
Fallible, resigned
to the unexpected.

A ghetto bird made laps above.
Gently, you taped Peruvian

butterflies in bubble wrap,
brittle wings kept whole.

MYSTERY

New York, NY 2005

The sad part is losing time,
And doing it again and again,

Knowing the end is laughably
The same.

Hardest thing to reteach a body.
Pleasure without danger

Seems implausible,
Unprecedented.

Power, the unknown,
The reckless surrender.

Arousal involves
An element of intrigue.

When I don't know
What the other is thinking,

I color them,
I bleed inside the lines.

COURTSHIP, 1944

for my grandfather Ambalal

On his way to Bombay, he meets a pretty girl.
They talk and she makes him tea.
Excited, he shows off his headshots.

Bombay. Everything he imagined.
The beach. The lights. Panipuri
late at night, tamarind-date sauce,
washed down with sugarcane juice,

young couples looking out
at the black space of the sea.

He decides to go to all the auditions.
Start with small parts in good pictures.
Everything happening slowly, of course,
everything unfolding exactly as it should.

He washes dishes, his Hindi improves,
he takes long walks, stares at the sea.

A letter arrives from the girl. He reads it
three times. Folds it up. Puts it away.
Reads it again the next morning:

Promised to write. Promised he was
different. Promised he would not forget her.
If he were a real man, he'd come back for her.

No niceties. All anger. Luminous.
Impressed, Ambalal marries
Santha, and becomes an accountant.

THE CONQUEST OF HAPPINESS

Boston, MA 2008—after a text by Bertrand Russell of the same title

JUDAS spray-painted on the concrete
    Pillar of the underpass. It's been so long
Since I watched autumn. All the red-white
    Leaves I've gathered, shown strangers,
Trying to find their name: *Excuse me,*
    Do you know what these are called?
A crabapple shucks off its yellow—
    Am I to believe this is happiness?
The train grinds on, a busted pane
    In the window of an old textile mill,
Smokestacks and spires until High Street,
    Where a star wrapped in an American
Flag hangs on a door. Onto ERNIE'S LUNCH
    HEAVENLY LICKS. *Conquest*
Of happiness, Russell reminds.
    Take the line of a spider's web, glinting.
What suspension! What tautness!
    Even if weed-whacked, itsy bitsy
Spins without delay. Martha Graham
    Said you must wake up and make
A list of everything that must be done,
    Then do it. But, she'd lock herself up,
Binge drinking long after creating
    Clytemnestra and *A Letter to the World.*
I make elaborate lists that I never
    Consult, writing them long after the

Things are done, simply to slash through
    To Do's with a red ergonomic pen.
Now my eye is in this graft of sky—
    Milk white, temporary, seen and dissolved,
And if resignation is essential to happiness,
    Then how far can the eye fall downward
Through train, mantle, and molten heat,
    Into a happiness, darting, aerodynamic?
Now I'm moving across water, or rather,
    The train is moving us all. Light leaps
Over green river onto a sidewalk thick with leaves.

GREEN

Haverhill, MA 2008

With a mind for late in life,
Negotiate your heart.

Overnight, the green.
Do I not know my own heart?

Grist of the body,
Grist of the mind.

The green is thick.
Rose hips and ferns.

At the bottom,
The pond has a plug.

Togetherness
Is a sequence

Of carefully
Orchestrated

Compromises.
I have forgotten

My snow heart.
Overnight, the green.

THE THIRD GENDER

Singers, dancers,
    happiest in motion,
the third gender
    knows the body
better than women do.

Swathed in color,
    painted faces,
they travel together,
    ready to perform.
Any minute
    comes word
of a birth. This morning,
    they visited

Santha who had a girl.
    Singing and
dancing hard to
    bring out mother
and child, they earned
    their keep for
celebrating birth but
    cloistered inside,
Santha would not come out.

Taunting, chanting,
　　　cursing the life
of the newborn Hemma,
　　　lifting their saris,
shoving bright folds
　　　into armpits. Limp,
hard, they stood waiting,
　　　cocks aired, a family.
She rushed out, she paid them.

SWEET MILK

for my mother, Hemma, born in 1947,
the year India won independence from British rule

Hemma high, no nipple for a thing that must
Be put down: dark, darker she grows

In sun, 1947 the year—hard
Is the suckle, Shiva clamps tit.

Only one love rules Santha.
1947. Autonomy. Under the lychee,

Hemma lies: face dried, guzzling
Bhang, sweeter than breast milk,

Bought by Santha to shut
Hemma up. Cloves, cardamom,

Cannabis leaves ground in cow's
Milk. Light wrings the lychee's

Leaves, light whips drupes.
The baby swallows vomit.

A neighbor calls the doctor.
If she dies, she dies.

A farmer stops scything,
Walks away from growth.

SLEEP, WAKE, SLEEP

Central Valley, CA 2009

Now you know to separate intuition
from paranoia. This is why you
look down or look away reflexively.
Down lies the earth, the trusted repository.
Away is a country with spectacle so seductive,
you become a voyeur, forgetting the self,
forgetting a self is even there to be forged.
It is a strange time, a strange new race:
the pundit sharing platitudes, the surgery-face
over-shares—their fifteen minutes continue
to be renewed. So many, in their silence,
absorbing trivia about people they've never
met. The throat is dry and the mare
at ease. In a fenced field, grass shorn,
soft and white. So much joy in this world.
The curved horns of the goat. The beavers'
gazebo, built of saplings gnawed to stumps.
One day, a rare gift: a kit fox in daylight
turns around, stares right through you.
Or does it? Do you discount your way of
knowing, of telling, assume it has failed?
A life burns, crystals form in its char.
Sometimes living filaments cut through—
the sky becomes a meadow, the world playfully
inverted. You run barefoot and your arches
rise below the brush of cumulus. Hills are

cloudy with scrub and starred with cattle.
The teats swollen, the udders inflamed.
You float into the slow and steady rise of
methane and the milk is drunk, and the cheese
hardens in its rind and you sleep, wake, sleep.

BUFFALO MILK

Jiba dips her fingers
In the white ghee
Of buffalo milk

To paint Hemma's feet.
Ghee from the farm!
A gift from her brother.

Slow, like a water buffalo,
Jiba strokes her heel,
Her arch, her ball.

And the village wives
Rubbing men's feet
Till they fall asleep.

LATE AFTERNOON
Boston, MA 2008

What you love are the patterns on grass—
tracing islands, rivulets, gullies through
shadows and light. You, a cartographer,
in the foreground of what could have been,
with the wind carrying cut grass. Parents
are rising to gather stuffed playthings
smelling of formula. Children turned
loose, cackling, crawling away—victories
played out before you. The office workers
plunked down, sweating in pantyhose,
eating bánh mi sandwiches over dog-
eared paperbacks. A musician sorting a
fiddle case of bills, a man reading the paper
out loud—his wife has escaped through a
smartphone. So many bodies converging,
scattering, stippled together through a day.
And the tacit agreements between body and
body, dissolving the self. Many years have
passed since you were last here. The hour is
long. Mallards shine, grass thins. If gravity
binds ambition, forget you are bound.
In your afterlife, the map unadulterated,
you'll speak in lucid tones, collapsing the
distance between who you thought you'd
become and who you always were.

HEMMA REMEMBERS TWO CITIES

A Charlie flat in Bombay
Where Father lavishes
Hours over his map:

Where to land, shore up,
And take on the life
Of a chartered

Accountant. Crustal
To the din of the dhaba
Stand. A mollusk

Marks Dar es Salaam
As pearled.

HEMMA REMEMBERS DISORDER

One night, one month
Before leaving for Africa,
A rat bit Father, he grew ill

And I grew ill from the smell
Of sweat, his body turning
On the cot as we waited

For his fever to end,
Our passports ready.

Finally my mother called a doctor.
He chastised her for waiting.
Told her if she'd waited any longer,
My father could have died,
There would have been no Africa.

Inconsolable, she accused me.
I had done it, possessed the rat.

It was comical. It was absurd.
The beginning of doubt,
Of obsession. It became true
The more I thought it through.

Small and faint, I kept
To the edge of her life.

HEMMA REMEMBERS SICKNESS

Father recovers,
We leave the Charlie flat,
Second-class on the ship.

Through the porthole of our cabin,
The blue steadfast for days.
Then comes a shore, wherein

I'm in the scratching
Of our Charlie walls.
Am I a sickness?

You tried to kill him—
She won't forgive.
Sorry sorry I say

Sorry three times,
Blink for each sorry,
Burn the Arabian Sea

Into my brain.
How powerful
I became,

Scurrying in dark,
I controlled the rat,
But what controlled me?

BOOTCAMP VIPASSANA

North Fork, CA 2007

4 a.m. gong. Nostrils, the upper lip. Capital of the face.
    Ten days of sitting, ten hours a day.
No Vigorous Exercise, so around the bog, I speed-walk.
    Who places raisins in the spider's web?
Silence At All Times, but they can't hear the ventriloquist in my head.
    Nighttime tapping, neighbor taking Xanax.
No Reading, so I dig up receipts. Did I buy scouring pads?
    I fantasize about full coverage including vision.
Dawn. Deer come out to watch us walk.
    What is it you *know*? Do you know trees? I know trees!
I sneak away, lie on rock. Granite lets one lie, expects nothing.
    Night. Sleeping under an ash. A moose?—no, a horse! Hooves past hair.
Constellations in strangers, a bluish cry.
    Women and men, separated, we circle the crown.
Mystery is short of breath. There is no beloved.

THE END OF SUMMER

Boston, MA 2008

That summer, you were deliberate in
all your actions. Neither young nor old,
you chose risk without trepidation.
The long summer days were cinched
minute by minute. Girls were hatched—
coming out younger and younger,
all dimples and earnest inquisition.
Now you could walk for hours and
flit in and out. When you smiled at a
stranger, you smiled with resolve.
When provoked, you were preternaturally
calm. Lettuce rippled, cherries bulged
under the pressure of touch. Babies were
teething. Their fathers in loose shirts
over paunches. Old men slurped oysters,
drank Beefeater martinis. Sometimes
the air smelled of lemon, sometimes of salt,
or garlic and ink, sometimes smelling
of a year that you thought you would
never remember. The streets contracted
and you walked through, anew. Summer
now centrifugal, whorled with light—
greener and greener and midway in life,
the mind seceded, its shadow dissolved.

II

RIVERS
Haverhill, MA 2008

You don't sleep a lot, you don't
Read what you should,
Like lots of Lucretius.

Look at you floating through a
Cardamom plant into wainscoting
Into the crabapple.

Look at you stroking a new river,
The Merrimack, shimmy
Up for a ripple.

Many sources—Rea, Msimbazi,
Swannonoa, Sabarmati,
Ganga, the Nile—

Muddle a mouth. Language you
Keep failing. Slowly losing
The first one.

Baby girl, *Na* went to *No*,
Zed turned *Zee*, *not* to *ain't*.
Asphalt you circled as the others

Played freeze tag and the Klan
Marched downtown in white sheets,
Determined to adopt a highway.

BIRMINGHAM, UK 1969

Snow coming down fast,
Hemma reading Tennyson,

Or trying to.
It's loud, the one voice that fills her.

Outside, people walking
On snow in dark coats.

Ambalal has said *No* to hospital,
Afraid that after shock therapy

Santha may lose her mind,
Hemma, lose her mother.

The street is quiet.
The street is white.

Hemma catches a bus,
Tennyson in her lap.

White segments, white rays,
Cars and awnings and then arriving.

A student stops her—"Why
Are you wearing slippers?"

Looking down
To green frogs at the end

Of legs in snow—it's true,
The feet are hers!

NIGHT WITH THE VICAR

Boston, MA 2008

The vicar had curled nails. Off came his cassock,
And I knew we'd canter far, pausing for baby raccoons
Who were gassy in snow. It warmed us, to laugh.
I had said *No* to an arranged marriage. Ice fell in
Great slabs and I touched the embers in the cast iron
Chimnea rearing itself through a drift. Into its black

Came the green of chaparral and we found ourselves
Under a coffered ceiling, with a supper laid out.
In the twilight, we ate Gouda and hot pickle, red ale
And rye, wished one another good night. Neither of us
Slept. He came to me, kissed me, long after I had told
My father. But that was years ago, I had aged.

My clavicles were soft now, my father had forgotten
My name. The vicar's kiss unbuckled my throat.
When I tried to walk, the wind threw me back
Into his lap—into me, seven days old, like a trussed
Chicken, kept alive, against my father's curled back.
Love I had not felt in a long time. The kiss resumed.

COURTSHIP, 1971

Half an hour to decide:
Hemma and the young suitor
Sent down the hall to chat.

Nothing he offered
Would be remembered.
She sat, thinking he is

A way out of Santha.
Sitting and thinking
In the orange frock

She'd been ordered
To wear, pulled off
A thrift store rack.

Mascara for lashes
Ridiculously long.
Beauty's loneliness

No one spoke of.
It seemed fair,
To ask for time.

THE NINTH MONTH

The ceiling light
Yellow and new,

Warming me over,
Bright above me.

That's her—my ma
Saying *Soon*.

Nights. We're alone.
I've learned to project.

In the black, I see grids,
Coordinates. Cities

Undulate, the body
Caves and I

Lift out,
Look down, afraid,

Distance bittersweet.
There I am,

Whole, inside,
Hand on her navel.

IN THE GARDEN

Ambalal liked the end of a workday,
Smoking in the garden, far from his wife.

Bees in peonies. Grass tall and silver.
His grandchild stood on his lap,

The toddler taking his hat,
Throwing it down, laughing.

He'd bend forward,
He'd put it back on.

Became a game with her,
Off and on and never a word—

So this was patience, he thought,
Unaffordable years ago:

Newly wed, his daughter calling
Daddy, please take me back.

SUNDAY
Los Angeles, CA 2001

A cobweb has fallen
onto the love seat
where I nap
and the ivory curtains
are, as always, drawn.

Darling thwarted angel,
Scratch a cumulus
through cracked glass
nursing on the
grace of mass.

FUNERAL

Ambalal lies
Asleep in his suit
On a white sheet.

Five years old, V
Squeezes his nose
To double-check.

The others laugh.
A silence in V.
Third eye

Transient,
A lash falling,
A nostril's flare.

THE POLYGAMIST'S BUTTONS

Pearly top two buttons of
The railway conductor's
Coat become earrings

Fashioned by Jiba,
His second wife,
After his stroke.

Bereavement
Is simple, involves
No words, no mention

Of dissolving
A husband's face,
A father's face.

In the year after,
Santha wakes early,
Braids her hair,

Inserts buttons
Of the railway
Into her ears.

After a while,
The buttons stay
Inside a box until

Hemma takes them
For her child.
The buttons

Clamp new ears,
Push into holes.
Lobes red, V

Stops wearing them,
Forgets they're hers,
Bored with jewelry.

HOO

"Hoo Choo" is a transliteration of the Gujarati expression for "It is I."

Who is it my grandfather murmurs.
Thieves answer, flawless Gujarati:
Hoo Choo and slip out. Only in
The morning does he discover an
Empty cash box and laughs. I tell

This story to a weeping willow in
Western Carolina, and I it is, I the *Hoo,*
Little thief in clutch, under monkey
Bars, miming, forgetting place, that
Fault where the river was a fountain

Called "The Floozy in the Jacuzzi."
Dangle *Hoo* harder, Mummy dog-
Eared the goal. What a sky I map
When I'm upside down, the cumuli
I once believed *Hoo'd* bounce on.

DICTIONARY

Hardback.
Its cover hurts my eyes:

Wordswordswords
In primary red and yellow.

Inside, the pages marked.
A box

Drawn around the double
Consonants in *accuse.*

Abbess and *abscess*
Also boxed.

Agony squiggled
Twice

For its soft guttural.
A, a brute vowel.

Mummy in bed,
Asks me to sit down, opens

An Easy Dictionary, charts long
Vowels with a red felt pen.

Th, a stumpy phoneme, beatific
When paired with a long *e*.

I write up
An order of words

5x each on graph paper.
A long night spent alone

With *An Easy Dictionary,*
On *bobbin bobbin,*

Nonsensical reprieve.
Late morning and the moon.

How can sun *appear* too?
Bonny not just a name.

Mummy not *bonny,*
Body tender to touch.

Nights. More rain.
Green roses at dusk,

A kitchen of red ants,
Caddy of loose tea.

THE LIBRARY SALE
after Wallace Stevens

My mother returned with books
She stacked on my bed.

I stayed faithful to
Nancy in the clear dark of a clock tower.

A mystery taking me into late night,
A mystery ending in morning.

Neighbors at church. A chalky sky.
Rusted poles of our swing set, I kept
Swinging until I tired of its squawk.

Terrible to come to the end of a series,
Unable to return to its beginning.

I tried an anthology, came to *Sunday Morning*—
I was in it! Deep in the illness of Sunday, I read

Complacencies of the peignoir.
What was this?
Something dirty, something lacy, something red,

Nancy Drew couldn't unravel this.
Strawberry blonde and a *cockatoo,*
Its feathers floating through my mother.

Green a *freedom.*
I looked at our yard.
Magnolia leaves, yellowed grass.

Something under my chest,
Leaves of words I didn't get,
A bubble of the soft palate.

Sepulchre sounded mad,
But not exactly a cuss word.

Context clues didn't do much for *dominion.*
I pictured dominoes, a game I'd never get,
And how much I liked dots, some lime green.

The instructions pointless, since I liked my way just fine,
Lining them in serpentine trails, and clacking them down.

And the *woman,* I kept returning to her—
Being little, being a girl was taking too long.
I wanted to be old now.

What I would be then, alone, away from this,
On a Sunday when I am grown,
With the fine spray of *oranges*
In my pores, in my throat of dark roast.

KAMLA

Gujarat, India 2007

The last time Kamla saw me,
The first time she saw me

As an adult, no longer
A child of seven,

I was now a woman
Forgetting birthdays.

I had stopped measuring,
Grateful to be here

With my grandmother
Who couldn't remember

How old she was—
She thought maybe 78.

We were drinking chai
In her blue house.

The street thick with mud,
The village emptied of girls,

And the skin on my tea
Pinched like the skin

Of her face, my hand
Drawn to its stretch over bone.

MARRIAGE

Light and shadows
On the old carriage house,

And the blue jay troughing
To steal a dove's egg.

This garden is laundered.
Husbands are useless.

V taught never to depend on a man,
Being raised like a boy.

Greenbacks. Blackflies. At the storm
Window, V stands, watching.

Lemon balm invasive, Hemma
Mulching. Her escarole glows.

SLEEPING IN THE WALMART LOT, 1996

A fight over a nativity set so Hemma returns it
And walks slowly back to the car, deciding

To fast again. See how long it takes this time to
Pass out. Streetlight and a confectionary snow.

Nebula spun for the fresh bruise of a cheek.
White reflects all. O to fall asleep in snow!

Father Christmas—no, what country are we in?
—*Santa* ringing his bell, takes her spare change.

The store closing soon, nativity returns to the shelf.
Trying to sleep in the car, she watches a man

Load bags into his trunk. He returns the cart.
He touches his wife lightly on the shoulder.

POMEGRANATE

When a woman has changed her clothes at the end of her menstrual period, a
man should approach that splendid woman and invite her to have sex. Should she
refuse to consent, he should bribe her. If she still refuses, he should beat her with
a stick or with his fists and overpower her, saying: "I take away the splendor from
you with my virility and splendor." —*Brhadaranyaka Upaniṣad 6.4.12*

Splendor in the twist
of cotton burning in ghee
as gods, marble and bronze,
bathed in whole milk,
marked vermilion,
pupil-less, smile on.

Also splendor in daily stories—
survival depends on stories,
the humbling of men as
forests swallow seasons,
the lost years
cawing through vines.

Splendor too in her fingers
opening a pomegranate,
rajas' favorite, Eden's apple,
darling of the underworld.
So here, now, buds flared,
teeth grinding seeds and

Splendor splendor,
tannic asides, seconds
so tart-sweet, tart-sweet,
as arils thrum
in recess, in darkness, in
viscous blood.

RAIN
Boston, MA 2008

Let's open a window.
Please. Can we listen
To it rain while we talk?

The table will get wet,
I'll wipe it before bed.

Electric, credit, heat,
Bills under an op-ed.

You speak, I hear,
My semantical Master.

Everyone everywhere is busy
In a young body. Relentless.

I want to be relentless,
While I still have time.

No matter who tends me,
Constancy of rain.

In that wet dark green,
Petals shine, and the only
Body the only lust
Is a small white wound

Captive with others,
Moving strangely.

CVS PHARMACY

Central Valley, CA 2009

You've come here to touch things: metallic lipstick, eye shadow in taupe,
A tub of pumice stones, silver glitter nail polish aptly titled "City Lights"—
Ah, this tramp was exquisitely deluded. Moreover, what a lousy detective you are.
O the circumstantial evidence amassed! O person of interest!
You were wrong to think you were right. You were wrong to ever *think* you could be
Right. Wrong, wrong just as everything here is wrong: this lipstick matte, not metallic.
That's not bath milk, babe, it's Drano. The bath milk is in that other CVS,
Another coast where you still did the math of equating sensation to truth. Now you're
Stuck. The clerk a sweet boy with a strong jaw, stocking shelves with yellow peeps,
Asks if you need help. Oh Christ—be decisive! Don't let yourself be marked.
Don't float in the aisles, or stand empty-handed, staring at dye kits. Make believe
That advantage is yours. Fill your house with boiled eggs glazed gold,
Spotted and pearled, objective and evidence, for you may exist, you may be right.

TIME

Central Valley, CA 2009

Tannhäuser starts your morning and when it stops,
the lowing of cattle startles you, sound newly plaintive—
that you live here, that the sandhill crane
can launch out of stillness, the wings sluicing air—
confirmation: surely you exist, but look now—
branches are cobwebs, the green birds caught.
Can you name each thing in time?
Prove it, prove you're not a dilettante.

'79 BMW STALLS AGAIN
Orange County, CA 2005

Henry's latest diagnosis: she needs a new
Catalytic converter. Almost broke,

He does his homework, goes online,
Bids on eBay, buys a respectable copy

Of Raphael's *Saint Cecilia* in a
Gold leaf frame, orders Roman denarii.

Collection Agents: CAPS LOCK means nothing.
Whatever you send is unopened, recycled.

His account is emptied. Nothing left to
Garnish. Marcus Aurelius is en route—

Something to hold, to unclench Henry's fist.
He drives her through the Mojave at a

100 mph. Bugs splatter the windshield.
Desert candles, fat and lit, bloom purple.

CITY AUBADE

Los Angeles, CA 2001

Birds strung on high-tension wires,
my tongue heavy in its thick hot nest,
I slip out. Arch Drive quiet.

Lily doing downward dog.
A few leaves float in the pool.
Arkady working on his children's
book with a message, about cats
in dogface in a minstrel show.

The convenience store where
I was asked to become an escort.
The cafe where paparazzi
camp out with telephoto lenses.

It's snowing. Rivers of fire
cut through mountains.
Chaparral burns, everyone
saying *hello, hello.* I try
to belong, to mimic sounds.

It's snowing. We wear masks.
We're all very nice. Sentient
beings, birds struck from the sky.

III

BOLL WEEVIL & THE MAKE OR BREAK

The family left, the field
Sheared, cotton flew
In great drifts blown
Skyward. Airborne fluff
In ashen contrails, in snowfall,
In disparate parts—where were we?
Sometimes we streamed through red,
Sometimes diffused in gold,
The white whitening and worn,
We thought *texture*, and the ghost went nit-nit,
We thought *contour,* and the ghost crawled.
Such pigeon-winging words. Such finagling—
Kettle Logic and if-by-whisky,
Straw man begged the question:
Who knew where we were flown?
Uganda, the Carolinas, California
Where the pink light saved the scavengers,
Where the pink light split the lip in suck.

BELIEF REVISION

for my grandfather Dahya

I.

14-years-old, Dahya boards a ship for Uganda—
The *Pearl* of Africa, to work as a day laborer,
to lift for the British. Elephant grass, swamp,
he's done with land, becomes a middleman,
after cholera takes his only brother.

All day, the farmers stand in long lines, Dahya
weighs the cotton, tosses it over his shoulder.
When the warehouse fills, he drives
a truck of fluff to the ginnery.

2.

Dahya orders his sons to stay outdoors, so
the boys hike forty times up Turoro Rock and camp,
cook curry, biking hundreds of miles. Grasslands,
papyrus, bush babies, the cries of hyenas at midnight,
the candelabra trees. To speak Swahili, and build
campfires in the world of white rhinos.

3.

1972: Big Daddy gives them ninety days to
clear out. *Indians! Go Home!* The streets emptied,
no one wanders outside. Amin's henchmen roam,
looting. To stay is to risk being rounded up for camps.

Auntie paints gold jewelry red—ring after ring
buried under cheap bangles in a biscuit tin.
They leave the house, the land, the weight
of cotton, drive through twenty-one road blocks.

Take it. Take the jewelry, Auntie insists.
The guard smirks, waves them on.

Waved them on: It could have been her skin, peeled,
fed to an alligator or Amin himself gnawing
on Auntie's thigh—so a story of the last
day relived, rewritten in the years ahead, the tellers
with tea, red darkening, the exit a bony thigh.

4.

At 72, Dahya visits his sons in London,
watches his granddaughters play: V and Anu
born a month apart, have never met this man,
Dada, so quiet he must hate them.

Anu's plump hand swats flies. She teaches V
not to be afraid of touching dead bodies, to marvel
at iridescence every time they smack one down.
Flat-footed V prances for Dada, clasping Anu's hand
and off they go! Skipping on parquet, ponytails swinging,
they neigh for Dada, who nurses warm beer.

    5.

Anu sent alone to Africa, to stay with family.
Afternoon, she comes back from the market with her
aunt and uncle, their arms full of pawpaw, jackfruit, yams,
sweet banana and a stranger in the kitchen kills
the uncle, then the aunt. Anu tensing, mangoes green
in puddles of red. Fifteen days and her body found floating
in an open sewer. Blood mattes her ponytail. Flesh flies.
The killer, long gone, in the world of white rhinos.

    6.

Dahya doesn't come to the wake. Auntie screams,
forehead on knees. Then comes next week—who are they,
the whole family conspiring to go on? To wake and scrape
white film off a tongue, chew fennel seeds to freshen breath,
sell stolen goods, count every pence, make wicks with cotton?
Auntie gives birth to two sons. By then, Dahya,
swallowing ulcer tablets, can't remember much of anything.
When he dies, his sons write notes: *Father died.*
Exactly which organ shut down, they soon forget.

7.

V recites facts, anecdotes, bits of gossip gleaned from grown-ups.
Compulsion to record. School doesn't teach you a way to do it.
When Mrs. Mulloy points at a kitty, all kindergartners
chant in unison: *Cuh Cuh Cuh.* Past midnight, V
smashes her face in down, tracking the curve—where
is Anu, where is Dada? London sour with the overflow
of exiles, sky a cemetery. Dada takes the end of Orion's Belt.
Fly Anu far into Milky Way suns, settle her
in green bronze under the great pillars of the Eagle Nebula.

If only Dada had set aside his beer to wave them closer,
let his hand come to rest on the small of Anu's back.

Tedious work to be almost six, revising the future,
making it touchable, an iridescent thing. Tensing to
make believe so grown-ups after shifts
of selling sweets to whites could open beers,
eat salt and vinegar crisps, watch evening
soaps, syndicated, from America.

NIGHT
Central Valley, CA 2009

Night. Night stretches.
The coyote pulls its tongue from the root.
The coyote wants the perch of the owl.
The owls have petrified on bark.

Blades of wild grass fall tender,
Curl gently around bared feet.
The rabbit's heart slows.
Deep in the earth, a twin world, a twin

Heart stunted in its first growth and
The laying down of forks.
You can smell the last supper—
Lavender floating with thyme, chervil, chives,

The tureen is vast with a savory broth.
The tongue after so much butter
Indivisible, melts into the mélange—
You eat and eat, you would not know,

You would not suspect that
Above such a cathedral of rock
With its jeweled enclaves,
Wild grasses stitch a fine down.

APPENDIX: FAMILY TREE[*]

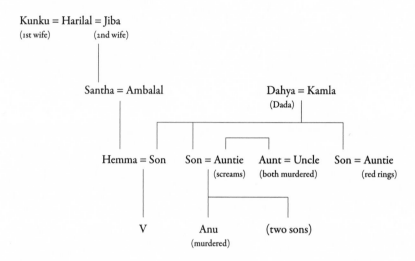

Kunku = Harilal = Jiba
(1st wife)   (2nd wife)

Santha = Ambalal

Dahya = Kamla
(Dada)

Hemma = Son   Son = Auntie   Aunt = Uncle   Son = Auntie
                      (screams)   (both murdered)   (red rings)

V   Anu   (two sons)
        (murdered)

KEY:

"=" represents marriage.

Horizontal lines represent sibling relations.

Vertical lines represent parent-child relations.

*This tree only presents that part of the family relevant to the poems, and names are only as explicit as in the poems themselves. Descriptive phrases to aid identification appear in parentheses.